40 Beef Jerky Recipes for Home

By: Kelly Johnson

Table of Contents

- Classic Teriyaki Beef Jerky
- Spicy Sriracha Beef Jerky
- Honey Garlic Beef Jerky
- Smoky Chipotle Beef Jerky
- Black Pepper & Garlic Beef Jerky
- Sweet BBQ Beef Jerky
- Asian Sesame Beef Jerky
- Cajun Beef Jerky
- Maple Glazed Beef Jerky
- Peppercorn & Soy Beef Jerky
- Honey Mustard Beef Jerky
- Red Wine & Garlic Beef Jerky
- Chili Lime Beef Jerky
- Bourbon BBQ Beef Jerky
- Garlic & Herb Beef Jerky
- Habanero Beef Jerky
- Pineapple Teriyaki Beef Jerky
- A1 Steak Sauce Beef Jerky
- Jalapeño & Cilantro Beef Jerky
- Sweet & Spicy Beef Jerky
- Lemon Pepper Beef Jerky
- Mustard & Brown Sugar Beef Jerky
- Worcestershire & Onion Beef Jerky
- Maple & Bacon Beef Jerky
- Thai Chili Beef Jerky
- Southwest Chipotle Beef Jerky
- Balsamic Vinegar Beef Jerky
- Ginger Soy Beef Jerky
- Smoky Mesquite Beef Jerky
- Curry Beef Jerky
- Sweet Teriyaki Beef Jerky
- Horseradish Beef Jerky

- Zesty Lemon Beef Jerky
- Chipotle & Lime Beef Jerky
- Espresso Beef Jerky
- Pineapple & Teriyaki Beef Jerky
- Korean BBQ Beef Jerky
- Spicy Tamarind Beef Jerky
- Molasses & Pepper Beef Jerky
- Garlic & Chili Beef Jerky

Classic Teriyaki Beef Jerky

- 2 lbs beef (top round or flank steak)
- 1/2 cup soy sauce
- 1/4 cup teriyaki sauce
- 1/4 cup brown sugar
- 2 tbsp honey
- 1 tbsp minced garlic
- 1 tbsp minced ginger
- 1/2 tsp black pepper
- 1/2 tsp red pepper flakes (optional)

1. Slice beef thinly against the grain.
2. Mix soy sauce, teriyaki sauce, brown sugar, honey, garlic, ginger, pepper, and red pepper flakes in a bowl.
3. Marinate beef in the mixture for at least 4 hours or overnight.
4. Drain and pat dry.
5. Arrange beef strips on a dehydrator tray or oven rack.
6. Dry at 160°F (71°C) for 6-8 hours until jerky is dry but still slightly pliable.

Spicy Sriracha Beef Jerky

- 2 lbs beef (flank steak or top round)
- 1/2 cup soy sauce
- 1/4 cup Sriracha sauce
- 1/4 cup brown sugar
- 2 tbsp rice vinegar
- 2 tbsp minced garlic
- 1 tbsp minced ginger
- 1 tsp black pepper
- 1/2 tsp red pepper flakes (optional for extra heat)

1. Slice beef thinly against the grain.
2. Combine soy sauce, Sriracha, brown sugar, rice vinegar, garlic, ginger, pepper, and red pepper flakes in a bowl.
3. Marinate beef in the mixture for at least 4 hours or overnight.
4. Drain and pat dry.
5. Arrange beef strips on a dehydrator tray or oven rack.
6. Dry at 160°F (71°C) for 6-8 hours until jerky is dry but still slightly pliable.

Honey Garlic Beef Jerky

- 2 lbs beef (flank steak or top round)
- 1/2 cup soy sauce
- 1/4 cup honey
- 3 tbsp minced garlic
- 2 tbsp brown sugar
- 1 tbsp apple cider vinegar
- 1 tsp black pepper
- 1/2 tsp onion powder

1. Slice beef thinly against the grain.
2. Mix soy sauce, honey, garlic, brown sugar, apple cider vinegar, pepper, and onion powder in a bowl.
3. Marinate beef in the mixture for at least 4 hours or overnight.
4. Drain and pat dry.
5. Arrange beef strips on a dehydrator tray or oven rack.
6. Dry at 160°F (71°C) for 6-8 hours until jerky is dry but still slightly pliable.

Enjoy the sweet and savory flavor!

Smoky Chipotle Beef Jerky

- 2 lbs beef (flank steak or top round)
- 1/2 cup soy sauce
- 1/4 cup apple cider vinegar
- 2 tbsp chipotle powder
- 2 tbsp smoked paprika
- 2 tbsp brown sugar
- 1 tbsp minced garlic
- 1 tbsp minced onion
- 1 tsp ground cumin
- 1/2 tsp black pepper

1. Slice beef thinly against the grain.
2. In a bowl, combine soy sauce, apple cider vinegar, chipotle powder, smoked paprika, brown sugar, garlic, onion, cumin, and black pepper.
3. Marinate beef in the mixture for at least 4 hours or overnight.
4. Drain and pat dry.
5. Arrange beef strips on a dehydrator tray or oven rack.
6. Dry at 160°F (71°C) for 6-8 hours until jerky is dry but still slightly pliable.

Enjoy the smoky and spicy flavor!

Black Pepper & Garlic Beef Jerky

- 2 lbs beef (flank steak or top round)
- 1/2 cup soy sauce
- 2 tbsp black pepper
- 2 tbsp minced garlic
- 2 tbsp brown sugar
- 1 tbsp Worcestershire sauce
- 1 tbsp apple cider vinegar
- 1 tsp onion powder

1. Slice beef thinly against the grain.
2. Mix soy sauce, black pepper, garlic, brown sugar, Worcestershire sauce, apple cider vinegar, and onion powder in a bowl.
3. Marinate beef in the mixture for at least 4 hours or overnight.
4. Drain and pat dry.
5. Arrange beef strips on a dehydrator tray or oven rack.
6. Dry at 160°F (71°C) for 6-8 hours until jerky is dry but still slightly pliable.

Enjoy the bold peppery and garlicky flavor!

Sweet BBQ Beef Jerky

- 2 lbs beef (flank steak or top round)
- 1/2 cup BBQ sauce
- 1/4 cup soy sauce
- 1/4 cup brown sugar
- 2 tbsp honey
- 1 tbsp apple cider vinegar
- 1 tbsp smoked paprika
- 1 tsp garlic powder
- 1/2 tsp onion powder
- 1/2 tsp black pepper

1. Slice beef thinly against the grain.
2. In a bowl, combine BBQ sauce, soy sauce, brown sugar, honey, apple cider vinegar, smoked paprika, garlic powder, onion powder, and black pepper.
3. Marinate beef in the mixture for at least 4 hours or overnight.
4. Drain and pat dry.
5. Arrange beef strips on a dehydrator tray or oven rack.
6. Dry at 160°F (71°C) for 6-8 hours until jerky is dry but still slightly pliable.

Asian Sesame Beef Jerky

- 1 lb beef (flank steak or top round), thinly sliced
- 1/4 cup soy sauce
- 1/4 cup sesame oil
- 2 tbsp brown sugar
- 2 tbsp rice vinegar
- 1 tbsp sesame seeds
- 1 tsp garlic powder
- 1 tsp ginger powder
- 1/2 tsp black pepper

Instructions:

1. Prepare Marinade: In a bowl, whisk together soy sauce, sesame oil, brown sugar, rice vinegar, sesame seeds, garlic powder, ginger powder, and black pepper.
2. Marinate Beef: Place beef slices in a resealable plastic bag or shallow dish. Pour marinade over the beef, ensuring all slices are well-coated. Seal and refrigerate for 4-6 hours, or overnight for best flavor.
3. Drain Beef: Remove beef slices from marinade and pat dry with paper towels to remove excess liquid.
4. Arrange for Drying: Lay beef slices in a single layer on dehydrator trays or a baking rack.
5. Dehydrate: Dehydrate at 160°F (70°C) for 4-6 hours, or until the jerky is dry and slightly pliable.

Cajun Beef Jerky

- 1 lb beef (flank steak or top round), thinly sliced
- 1/4 cup soy sauce
- 2 tbsp Cajun seasoning
- 1 tbsp brown sugar
- 1 tbsp smoked paprika
- 1 tsp garlic powder
- 1/2 tsp black pepper

Instructions:

1. Prepare Marinade: In a bowl, mix together soy sauce, Cajun seasoning, brown sugar, smoked paprika, garlic powder, and black pepper.
2. Marinate Beef: Add beef slices to the marinade, ensuring each piece is well-coated. Marinate in the refrigerator for 4-6 hours.
3. Drain Beef: Remove slices from marinade and pat dry with paper towels.
4. Arrange for Drying: Place beef slices in a single layer on dehydrator trays or a baking rack.
5. Dehydrate: Dehydrate at 160°F (70°C) for 4-6 hours, or until the jerky is fully dried but still slightly flexible.

Maple Glazed Beef Jerky

- 1 lb beef (flank steak or top round), thinly sliced
- 1/4 cup soy sauce
- 1/4 cup pure maple syrup
- 2 tbsp brown sugar
- 1 tbsp garlic powder
- 1/2 tsp black pepper

Instructions:

1. Prepare Marinade: In a bowl, combine soy sauce, maple syrup, brown sugar, garlic powder, and black pepper.
2. Marinate Beef: Add beef slices to the marinade and ensure they are well-coated. Refrigerate for 4-6 hours or overnight.
3. Drain Beef: Remove beef from marinade and pat dry with paper towels.
4. Arrange for Drying: Lay beef slices out on dehydrator trays or a baking rack.
5. Dehydrate: Dehydrate at 160°F (70°C) for 4-6 hours, or until the jerky is dry and slightly chewy.

Peppercorn & Soy Beef Jerky

- 1 lb beef (flank steak or top round), thinly sliced
- 1/4 cup soy sauce
- 2 tbsp cracked black peppercorns
- 2 tbsp brown sugar
- 1 tbsp garlic powder
- 1/2 tsp onion powder

Instructions:

1. Prepare Marinade: Mix soy sauce, cracked black peppercorns, brown sugar, garlic powder, and onion powder in a bowl.
2. Marinate Beef: Add beef slices to the marinade, making sure each piece is well-coated. Marinate in the refrigerator for 4-6 hours.
3. Drain Beef: Remove beef slices from marinade and pat dry with paper towels.
4. Arrange for Drying: Place beef slices on dehydrator trays or a baking rack.
5. Dehydrate: Dehydrate at 160°F (70°C) for 4-6 hours, or until the jerky is dry and flexible.

Honey Mustard Beef Jerky

- 1 lb beef (flank steak or top round), thinly sliced
- 1/4 cup soy sauce
- 2 tbsp honey
- 2 tbsp Dijon mustard
- 1 tbsp brown sugar
- 1 tsp garlic powder
- 1/2 tsp black pepper

Instructions:

1. Prepare Marinade: In a bowl, whisk together soy sauce, honey, Dijon mustard, brown sugar, garlic powder, and black pepper.
2. Marinate Beef: Add beef slices to the marinade and mix well. Refrigerate for 4-6 hours.
3. Drain Beef: Remove slices from marinade and pat dry with paper towels.
4. Arrange for Drying: Lay beef slices in a single layer on dehydrator trays or a baking rack.
5. Dehydrate: Dehydrate at 160°F (70°C) for 4-6 hours, or until the jerky is fully dried and slightly chewy.

Red Wine & Garlic Beef Jerky

- 1 lb beef (flank steak or top round), thinly sliced
- 1/4 cup soy sauce
- 1/4 cup red wine
- 2 tbsp brown sugar
- 1 tbsp garlic powder
- 1 tsp onion powder
- 1/2 tsp black pepper

Instructions:

1. Prepare Marinade: Mix soy sauce, red wine, brown sugar, garlic powder, onion powder, and black pepper in a bowl.
2. Marinate Beef: Add beef slices to the marinade, ensuring they are well-coated. Refrigerate for 4-6 hours or overnight.
3. Drain Beef: Remove beef slices from marinade and pat dry with paper towels.
4. Arrange for Drying: Place beef slices in a single layer on dehydrator trays or a baking rack.
5. Dehydrate: Dehydrate at 160°F (70°C) for 4-6 hours, or until the jerky is dry and slightly chewy.

Chili Lime Beef Jerky

- 1 lb beef (flank steak or top round), thinly sliced
- 1/4 cup soy sauce
- 2 tbsp lime juice
- 2 tbsp chili powder
- 2 tbsp brown sugar
- 1 tsp garlic powder
- 1/2 tsp black pepper

Instructions:

1. Prepare Marinade: Combine soy sauce, lime juice, chili powder, brown sugar, garlic powder, and black pepper in a bowl.
2. Marinate Beef: Add beef slices to the marinade, ensuring all pieces are well-coated. Marinate in the refrigerator for 4-6 hours.
3. Drain Beef: Remove beef from marinade and pat dry with paper towels.
4. Arrange for Drying: Lay beef slices on dehydrator trays or a baking rack.
5. Dehydrate: Dehydrate at 160°F (70°C) for 4-6 hours, or until the jerky is dry and slightly pliable.

Bourbon BBQ Beef Jerky

- 1 lb beef (flank steak or top round), thinly sliced
- 1/4 cup BBQ sauce
- 1/4 cup bourbon
- 2 tbsp brown sugar
- 1 tbsp smoked paprika
- 1 tsp garlic powder
- 1/2 tsp black pepper

Instructions:

1. Prepare Marinade: Mix BBQ sauce, bourbon, brown sugar, smoked paprika, garlic powder, and black pepper in a bowl.
2. Marinate Beef: Add beef slices to the marinade, ensuring they are well-coated. Marinate in the refrigerator for 4-6 hours or overnight.
3. Drain Beef: Remove beef slices from marinade and pat dry with paper towels.
4. Arrange for Drying: Place beef slices on dehydrator trays or a baking rack.
5. Dehydrate: Dehydrate at 160°F (70°C) for 4-6 hours, or until the jerky is dry and flexible.

Garlic & Herb Beef Jerky

- 1 lb beef (flank steak or top round), thinly sliced
- 1/4 cup soy sauce
- 2 tbsp dried herbs (thyme, oregano, rosemary)
- 2 tbsp garlic powder
- 1 tbsp brown sugar
- 1/2 tsp black pepper

Instructions:

1. Prepare Marinade: Combine soy sauce, dried herbs, garlic powder, brown sugar, and black pepper in a bowl.
2. Marinate Beef: Add beef slices to the marinade, ensuring each piece is well-coated. Marinate in the refrigerator for 4-6 hours.
3. Drain Beef: Remove beef slices from marinade and pat dry with paper towels.
4. Arrange for Drying: Lay beef slices out on dehydrator trays or a baking rack.
5. Dehydrate: Dehydrate at 160°F (70°C) for 4-6 hours, or until the jerky is fully dried and slightly chewy.

Habanero Beef Jerky

- 1 lb beef (flank steak or top round), thinly sliced
- 1/4 cup soy sauce
- 2 tbsp habanero hot sauce
- 2 tbsp brown sugar
- 1 tbsp garlic powder
- 1/2 tsp black pepper

Instructions:

1. Prepare Marinade: In a bowl, mix soy sauce, habanero hot sauce, brown sugar, garlic powder, and black pepper.
2. Marinate Beef: Add beef slices to the marinade, ensuring each piece is well-coated. Marinate in the refrigerator for 4-6 hours.
3. Drain Beef: Remove beef slices from marinade and pat dry with paper towels.
4. Arrange for Drying: Lay beef slices on dehydrator trays or a baking rack.
5. Dehydrate: Dehydrate at 160°F (70°C) for 4-6 hours, or until the jerky is dry and flexible.

Pineapple Teriyaki Beef Jerky

- 1 lb beef (flank steak or top round), thinly sliced
- 1/4 cup soy sauce
- 1/4 cup pineapple juice
- 2 tbsp teriyaki sauce
- 2 tbsp brown sugar
- 1 tsp garlic powder
- 1/2 tsp black pepper

Instructions:

1. Prepare Marinade: In a bowl, mix soy sauce, pineapple juice, teriyaki sauce, brown sugar, garlic powder, and black pepper.
2. Marinate Beef: Add beef slices to the marinade, ensuring they are well-coated. Refrigerate for 4-6 hours or overnight.
3. Drain Beef: Remove beef slices from marinade and pat dry with paper towels.
4. Arrange for Drying: Place beef slices on dehydrator trays or a baking rack.
5. Dehydrate: Dehydrate at 160°F (70°C) for 4-6 hours, or until the jerky is dry and slightly chewy.

A1 Steak Sauce Beef Jerky

- 1 lb beef (flank steak or top round), thinly sliced
- 1/4 cup A1 steak sauce
- 1/4 cup soy sauce
- 2 tbsp brown sugar
- 1 tbsp garlic powder
- 1/2 tsp black pepper

Instructions:

1. Prepare Marinade: Combine A1 steak sauce, soy sauce, brown sugar, garlic powder, and black pepper in a bowl.
2. Marinate Beef: Add beef slices to the marinade, ensuring each piece is well-coated. Marinate in the refrigerator for 4-6 hours.
3. Drain Beef: Remove beef slices from marinade and pat dry with paper towels.
4. Arrange for Drying: Lay beef slices out on dehydrator trays or a baking rack.
5. Dehydrate: Dehydrate at 160°F (70°C) for 4-6 hours, or until the jerky is dry and slightly pliable.

Jalapeño & Cilantro Beef Jerky

- 1 lb beef (flank steak or top round), thinly sliced
- 1/4 cup soy sauce
- 2 tbsp chopped fresh cilantro
- 2 tbsp jalapeño pepper sauce
- 1 tbsp lime juice
- 1 tbsp brown sugar
- 1 tsp garlic powder
- 1/2 tsp black pepper

Instructions:

1. Prepare Marinade: In a bowl, mix soy sauce, chopped cilantro, jalapeño pepper sauce, lime juice, brown sugar, garlic powder, and black pepper.
2. Marinate Beef: Add beef slices to the marinade, ensuring they are well-coated. Marinate in the refrigerator for 4-6 hours or overnight.
3. Drain Beef: Remove beef slices from marinade and pat dry with paper towels.
4. Arrange for Drying: Place beef slices on dehydrator trays or a baking rack.
5. Dehydrate: Dehydrate at 160°F (70°C) for 4-6 hours, or until the jerky is dry and slightly chewy.

Sweet & Spicy Beef Jerky

- 1 lb beef (flank steak or top round), thinly sliced
- 1/4 cup soy sauce
- 2 tbsp honey
- 1 tbsp sriracha or hot sauce
- 2 tbsp brown sugar
- 1 tsp garlic powder
- 1/2 tsp black pepper

Instructions:

1. Prepare Marinade: In a bowl, whisk together soy sauce, honey, sriracha, brown sugar, garlic powder, and black pepper.
2. Marinate Beef: Add beef slices to the marinade, making sure they are well-coated. Refrigerate for 4-6 hours or overnight.
3. Drain Beef: Remove beef slices from marinade and pat dry with paper towels.
4. Arrange for Drying: Lay beef slices in a single layer on dehydrator trays or a baking rack.
5. Dehydrate: Dehydrate at 160°F (70°C) for 4-6 hours, or until the jerky is dry and slightly pliable.

Lemon Pepper Beef Jerky

- 1 lb beef (flank steak or top round), thinly sliced
- 1/4 cup soy sauce
- 2 tbsp lemon juice
- 2 tbsp cracked black pepper
- 1 tbsp brown sugar
- 1 tsp garlic powder

Instructions:

1. Prepare Marinade: In a bowl, combine soy sauce, lemon juice, cracked black pepper, brown sugar, and garlic powder.
2. Marinate Beef: Add beef slices to the marinade, ensuring each piece is well-coated. Marinate in the refrigerator for 4-6 hours or overnight.
3. Drain Beef: Remove beef slices from marinade and pat dry with paper towels.
4. Arrange for Drying: Place beef slices on dehydrator trays or a baking rack.
5. Dehydrate: Dehydrate at 160°F (70°C) for 4-6 hours, or until the jerky is dry and slightly chewy.

Mustard & Brown Sugar Beef Jerky

- 1 lb beef (flank steak or top round), thinly sliced
- 1/4 cup soy sauce
- 2 tbsp yellow mustard
- 2 tbsp brown sugar
- 1 tbsp apple cider vinegar
- 1 tsp garlic powder
- 1/2 tsp black pepper

Instructions:

1. Prepare Marinade: Mix soy sauce, yellow mustard, brown sugar, apple cider vinegar, garlic powder, and black pepper in a bowl.
2. Marinate Beef: Add beef slices to the marinade, making sure they are well-coated. Marinate in the refrigerator for 4-6 hours or overnight.
3. Drain Beef: Remove beef slices from marinade and pat dry with paper towels.
4. Arrange for Drying: Lay beef slices out on dehydrator trays or a baking rack.
5. Dehydrate: Dehydrate at 160°F (70°C) for 4-6 hours, or until the jerky is dry and flexible.

Worcestershire & Onion Beef Jerky

- 1 lb beef (flank steak or top round), thinly sliced
- 1/4 cup soy sauce
- 2 tbsp Worcestershire sauce
- 2 tbsp dried onion flakes
- 2 tbsp brown sugar
- 1 tsp garlic powder
- 1/2 tsp black pepper

Instructions:

1. Prepare Marinade: Combine soy sauce, Worcestershire sauce, dried onion flakes, brown sugar, garlic powder, and black pepper in a bowl.
2. Marinate Beef: Add beef slices to the marinade, ensuring they are well-coated. Refrigerate for 4-6 hours or overnight.
3. Drain Beef: Remove beef slices from marinade and pat dry with paper towels.
4. Arrange for Drying: Place beef slices on dehydrator trays or a baking rack.
5. Dehydrate: Dehydrate at 160°F (70°C) for 4-6 hours, or until the jerky is dry and slightly chewy.

Maple & Bacon Beef Jerky

- 1 lb beef (flank steak or top round), thinly sliced
- 1/4 cup soy sauce
- 2 tbsp pure maple syrup
- 2 tbsp crumbled cooked bacon
- 1 tbsp brown sugar
- 1 tsp garlic powder
- 1/2 tsp black pepper

Instructions:

1. Prepare Marinade: In a bowl, mix soy sauce, maple syrup, crumbled bacon, brown sugar, garlic powder, and black pepper.
2. Marinate Beef: Add beef slices to the marinade, ensuring they are well-coated. Marinate in the refrigerator for 4-6 hours or overnight.
3. Drain Beef: Remove beef slices from marinade and pat dry with paper towels.
4. Arrange for Drying: Lay beef slices on dehydrator trays or a baking rack.
5. Dehydrate: Dehydrate at 160°F (70°C) for 4-6 hours, or until the jerky is dry and slightly chewy.

Thai Chili Beef Jerky

- 1 lb beef (flank steak or top round), thinly sliced
- 1/4 cup soy sauce
- 2 tbsp Thai chili paste
- 2 tbsp brown sugar
- 1 tbsp lime juice
- 1 tsp garlic powder
- 1/2 tsp black pepper

Instructions:

1. Prepare Marinade: In a bowl, combine soy sauce, Thai chili paste, brown sugar, lime juice, garlic powder, and black pepper.
2. Marinate Beef: Add beef slices to the marinade, ensuring they are well-coated. Marinate in the refrigerator for 4-6 hours or overnight.
3. Drain Beef: Remove beef slices from marinade and pat dry with paper towels.
4. Arrange for Drying: Place beef slices on dehydrator trays or a baking rack.
5. Dehydrate: Dehydrate at 160°F (70°C) for 4-6 hours, or until the jerky is dry and slightly pliable.

Southwest Chipotle Beef Jerky

- 1 lb beef (flank steak or top round), thinly sliced
- 1/4 cup soy sauce
- 2 tbsp chipotle peppers in adobo sauce
- 2 tbsp brown sugar
- 1 tbsp lime juice
- 1 tsp garlic powder
- 1/2 tsp cumin

Instructions:

1. Prepare Marinade: In a bowl, mix soy sauce, chipotle peppers in adobo sauce, brown sugar, lime juice, garlic powder, and cumin.
2. Marinate Beef: Add beef slices to the marinade, ensuring they are well-coated. Marinate in the refrigerator for 4-6 hours or overnight.
3. Drain Beef: Remove beef slices from marinade and pat dry with paper towels.
4. Arrange for Drying: Lay beef slices on dehydrator trays or a baking rack.
5. Dehydrate. Dehydrate at 160°F (70°C) for 4-6 hours, or until the jerky is dry and slightly chewy.

Balsamic Vinegar Beef Jerky

- 1 lb beef (flank steak or top round), thinly sliced
- 1/4 cup soy sauce
- 2 tbsp balsamic vinegar
- 2 tbsp brown sugar
- 1 tbsp garlic powder
- 1/2 tsp black pepper

Instructions:

1. Prepare Marinade: Mix soy sauce, balsamic vinegar, brown sugar, garlic powder, and black pepper in a bowl.
2. Marinate Beef: Add beef slices to the marinade, ensuring they are well-coated. Refrigerate for 4-6 hours or overnight.
3. Drain Beef: Remove beef slices from marinade and pat dry with paper towels.
4. Arrange for Drying: Place beef slices on dehydrator trays or a baking rack.
5. Dehydrate: Dehydrate at 160°F (70°C) for 4-6 hours, or until the jerky is dry and slightly chewy.

Ginger Soy Beef Jerky

- 1 lb beef (flank steak or top round), thinly sliced
- 1/4 cup soy sauce
- 2 tbsp fresh ginger, minced
- 2 tbsp brown sugar
- 1 tbsp rice vinegar
- 1 tsp garlic powder
- 1/2 tsp black pepper

Instructions:

1. Prepare Marinade: In a bowl, combine soy sauce, minced ginger, brown sugar, rice vinegar, garlic powder, and black pepper.
2. Marinate Beef: Add beef slices to the marinade, ensuring they are well-coated. Marinate in the refrigerator for 4-6 hours or overnight.
3. Drain Beef: Remove beef slices from marinade and pat dry with paper towels.
4. Arrange for Drying: Lay beef slices on dehydrator trays or a baking rack.
5. Dehydrate: Dehydrate at 160°F (70°C) for 4-6 hours, or until the jerky is dry and slightly chewy.

Smoky Mesquite Beef Jerky

- 1 lb beef (flank steak or top round), thinly sliced
- 1/4 cup soy sauce
- 2 tbsp mesquite liquid smoke
- 2 tbsp brown sugar
- 1 tbsp smoked paprika
- 1 tsp garlic powder
- 1/2 tsp black pepper

Instructions:

1. Prepare Marinade: In a bowl, mix soy sauce, mesquite liquid smoke, brown sugar, smoked paprika, garlic powder, and black pepper.
2. Marinate Beef: Add beef slices to the marinade, making sure they are well-coated. Marinate in the refrigerator for 4-6 hours or overnight.
3. Drain Beef: Remove beef slices from marinade and pat dry with paper towels.
4. Arrange for Drying: Place beef slices on dehydrator trays or a baking rack.
5. Dehydrate: Dehydrate at 160°F (70°C) for 4-6 hours, or until the jerky is dry and slightly chewy.

Curry Beef Jerky

- 1 lb beef (flank steak or top round), thinly sliced
- 1/4 cup soy sauce
- 2 tbsp curry powder
- 2 tbsp brown sugar
- 1 tbsp apple cider vinegar
- 1 tsp garlic powder
- 1/2 tsp black pepper

Instructions:

1. Prepare Marinade: Combine soy sauce, curry powder, brown sugar, apple cider vinegar, garlic powder, and black pepper in a bowl.
2. Marinate Beef: Add beef slices to the marinade, ensuring they are well-coated. Marinate in the refrigerator for 4-6 hours or overnight.
3. Drain Beef: Remove beef slices from marinade and pat dry with paper towels.
4. Arrange for Drying: Lay beef slices out on dehydrator trays or a baking rack.
5. Dehydrate: Dehydrate at 160°F (70°C) for 4-6 hours, or until the jerky is fully dried and slightly chewy.

Sweet Teriyaki Beef Jerky

- 1 lb beef (flank steak or top round), thinly sliced
- 1/4 cup soy sauce
- 1/4 cup teriyaki sauce
- 2 tbsp brown sugar
- 1 tbsp honey
- 1 tsp garlic powder
- 1/2 tsp black pepper

Instructions:

1. Prepare Marinade: In a bowl, mix soy sauce, teriyaki sauce, brown sugar, honey, garlic powder, and black pepper.
2. Marinate Beef: Add beef slices to the marinade, ensuring each piece is well-coated. Marinate in the refrigerator for 4-6 hours or overnight.
3. Drain Beef: Remove beef slices from marinade and pat dry with paper towels.
4. Arrange for Drying: Place beef slices on dehydrator trays or a baking rack.
5. Dehydrate: Dehydrate at 160°F (70°C) for 4-6 hours, or until the jerky is dry and slightly chewy.

Horseradish Beef Jerky

- 1 lb beef (flank steak or top round), thinly sliced
- 1/4 cup soy sauce
- 2 tbsp prepared horseradish
- 2 tbsp brown sugar
- 1 tbsp apple cider vinegar
- 1 tsp garlic powder
- 1/2 tsp black pepper

Instructions:

1. Prepare Marinade: In a bowl, combine soy sauce, prepared horseradish, brown sugar, apple cider vinegar, garlic powder, and black pepper.
2. Marinate Beef: Add beef slices to the marinade, making sure they are well-coated. Marinate in the refrigerator for 4-6 hours or overnight.
3. Drain Beef: Remove beef slices from marinade and pat dry with paper towels.
4. Arrange for Drying: Lay beef slices on dehydrator trays or a baking rack.
5. Dehydrate: Dehydrate at 160°F (70°C) for 4-6 hours, or until the jerky is dry and slightly chewy.

Zesty Lemon Beef Jerky

- 1 lb beef (flank steak or top round), thinly sliced
- 1/4 cup soy sauce
- 2 tbsp lemon juice
- 2 tbsp lemon zest
- 2 tbsp brown sugar
- 1 tsp garlic powder
- 1/2 tsp black pepper

Instructions:

1. Prepare Marinade: Combine soy sauce, lemon juice, lemon zest, brown sugar, garlic powder, and black pepper in a bowl.
2. Marinate Beef: Add beef slices to the marinade, ensuring each piece is well-coated. Marinate in the refrigerator for 4-6 hours or overnight.
3. Drain Beef: Remove beef slices from marinade and pat dry with paper towels.
4. Arrange for Drying: Place beef slices on dehydrator trays or a baking rack.
5. Dehydrate: Dehydrate at 160°F (70°C) for 4-6 hours, or until the jerky is dry and slightly chewy.

Chipotle & Lime Beef Jerky

- 1 lb beef (flank steak or top round), thinly sliced
- 1/4 cup soy sauce
- 2 tbsp chipotle peppers in adobo sauce
- 2 tbsp lime juice
- 2 tbsp brown sugar
- 1 tsp garlic powder
- 1/2 tsp black pepper

Instructions:

1. Prepare Marinade: In a bowl, mix soy sauce, chipotle peppers in adobo sauce, lime juice, brown sugar, garlic powder, and black pepper.
2. Marinate Beef: Add beef slices to the marinade, making sure they are well-coated. Marinate in the refrigerator for 4-6 hours or overnight.
3. Drain Beef: Remove beef slices from marinade and pat dry with paper towels.
4. Arrange for Drying: Lay beef slices on dehydrator trays or a baking rack.
5. Dehydrate: Dehydrate at 160°F (70°C) for 4-6 hours, or until the jerky is dry and slightly pliable.

Espresso Beef Jerky

- 1 lb beef (flank steak or top round), thinly sliced
- 1/4 cup soy sauce
- 2 tbsp espresso coffee (brewed or instant)
- 2 tbsp brown sugar
- 1 tbsp Worcestershire sauce
- 1 tsp garlic powder
- 1/2 tsp black pepper

Instructions:

1. Prepare Marinade: In a bowl, mix soy sauce, espresso coffee, brown sugar, Worcestershire sauce, garlic powder, and black pepper.
2. Marinate Beef: Add beef slices to the marinade, making sure each piece is well-coated. Marinate in the refrigerator for 4-6 hours or overnight.
3. Drain Beef: Remove beef slices from marinade and pat dry with paper towels.
4. Arrange for Drying: Lay beef slices on dehydrator trays or a baking rack.
5. Dehydrate: Dehydrate at 160°F (70°C) for 4-6 hours, or until the jerky is dry and slightly chewy.

Pineapple & Teriyaki Beef Jerky

- 1 lb beef (flank steak or top round), thinly sliced
- 1/4 cup soy sauce
- 1/4 cup pineapple juice
- 2 tbsp teriyaki sauce
- 2 tbsp brown sugar
- 1 tsp garlic powder
- 1/2 tsp black pepper

Instructions:

1. Prepare Marinade: In a bowl, combine soy sauce, pineapple juice, teriyaki sauce, brown sugar, garlic powder, and black pepper.
2. Marinate Beef: Add beef slices to the marinade, ensuring they are well-coated. Refrigerate for 4-6 hours or overnight.
3. Drain Beef: Remove beef slices from marinade and pat dry with paper towels.
4. Arrange for Drying: Place beef slices on dehydrator trays or a baking rack.
5. Dehydrate: Dehydrate at 160°F (70°C) for 4-6 hours, or until the jerky is dry and slightly chewy.

Korean BBQ Beef Jerky

- 1 lb beef (flank steak or top round), thinly sliced
- 1/4 cup soy sauce
- 2 tbsp Korean BBQ sauce
- 2 tbsp brown sugar
- 1 tbsp sesame oil
- 1 tsp garlic powder
- 1/2 tsp black pepper

Instructions:

1. Prepare Marinade: Mix soy sauce, Korean BBQ sauce, brown sugar, sesame oil, garlic powder, and black pepper in a bowl.
2. Marinate Beef: Add beef slices to the marinade, ensuring each piece is well-coated. Marinate in the refrigerator for 4-6 hours or overnight.
3. Drain Beef: Remove beef slices from marinade and pat dry with paper towels.
4. Arrange for Drying: Lay beef slices out on dehydrator trays or a baking rack.
5. Dehydrate: Dehydrate at 160°F (70°C) for 4-6 hours, or until the jerky is dry and slightly pliable.

Spicy Tamarind Beef Jerky

- 1 lb beef (flank steak or top round), thinly sliced
- 1/4 cup soy sauce
- 2 tbsp tamarind paste
- 2 tbsp brown sugar
- 1 tbsp hot sauce
- 1 tsp garlic powder
- 1/2 tsp black pepper

Instructions:

1. Prepare Marinade: In a bowl, mix soy sauce, tamarind paste, brown sugar, hot sauce, garlic powder, and black pepper.
2. Marinate Beef: Add beef slices to the marinade, ensuring they are well-coated. Marinate in the refrigerator for 4-6 hours or overnight.
3. Drain Beef: Remove beef slices from marinade and pat dry with paper towels.
4. Arrange for Drying: Place beef slices on dehydrator trays or a baking rack.
5. Dehydrate: Dehydrate at 160°F (70°C) for 4-6 hours, or until the jerky is dry and slightly chewy.

Molasses & Pepper Beef Jerky

- 1 lb beef (flank steak or top round), thinly sliced
- 1/4 cup soy sauce
- 2 tbsp molasses
- 2 tbsp brown sugar
- 1 tbsp black pepper
- 1 tsp garlic powder

Instructions:

1. Prepare Marinade: Combine soy sauce, molasses, brown sugar, black pepper, and garlic powder in a bowl.
2. Marinate Beef: Add beef slices to the marinade, ensuring they are well-coated. Refrigerate for 4-6 hours or overnight.
3. Drain Beef: Remove beef slices from marinade and pat dry with paper towels.
4. Arrange for Drying: Lay beef slices on dehydrator trays or a baking rack.
5. Dehydrate: Dehydrate at 160°F (70°C) for 4-6 hours, or until the jerky is dry and slightly chewy.

Garlic & Chili Beef Jerky

- 1 lb beef (flank steak or top round), thinly sliced
- 1/4 cup soy sauce
- 2 tbsp chili garlic sauce
- 2 tbsp brown sugar
- 1 tbsp rice vinegar
- 1 tsp garlic powder
- 1/2 tsp black pepper

Instructions:

1. Prepare Marinade: Mix soy sauce, chili garlic sauce, brown sugar, rice vinegar, garlic powder, and black pepper in a bowl.
2. Marinate Beef: Add beef slices to the marinade, ensuring each piece is well-coated. Marinate in the refrigerator for 4-6 hours or overnight.
3. Drain Beef: Remove beef slices from marinade and pat dry with paper towels.
4. Arrange for Drying: Place beef slices on dehydrator trays or a baking rack.
5. Dehydrate: Dehydrate at 160°F (70°C) for 4-6 hours, or until the jerky is dry and slightly chewy.